AF516218

Rang Leela

A Collection of Poems

notionpress.com

Rang Leela

A Collection of Poems

Piyush 'Jayant' Arora

notionpress.com

Notion Press

5 Muthu Kalathy Street, Triplicane,

Chennai - 600 005

First Published by Notion Press 2015

ISBN: 978-93-52060-22-1

To my family,

for always being there for me…

Preface

Nah... It's not the sun,
For it rises and sets everyday...

It's not the tide,
For it wets the same shore repeatedly...

It's not the tree,
For it grows at the same place forever...

It's you my friend... Yes you!!
Amongst all the great prisoners of nature,
You are bestowed to break the monotony...

Human mind is infinitely creative! It has the power to imagine and then create the imagined. It takes you across continents and in the inner realms of human nature at the same time. I have been out on this journey from the last 7 years. Now I want to take you along on this journey called 'LIFE' through this book. Lets break the monotony!

The destination is still not in sight. Maybe, it will never be...

Piyush 'Jayant' Arora
28th March 2015
New Delhi

ACKNOWLEDGEMENT

This book is a product of numerous experiences and interactions over the last many years and an 'Acknowledgments' section cannot do justice to all those involved. However, I would like to mention a few names who have contributed immensely to this journey.

First and foremost, I want to thank GOD for everything that has ever happened in my life.

I want to thank my parents (Sunil and Saroj Arora) for always letting me do what I truly felt was my calling. I also want to thank my wife, Varidhi, for being my first reader cum editor and bearing with me all the time I spent alone with my thoughts. I am also grateful to my brother, Rohan for his inputs and my in-laws (Gossain family) for always being supportive.

This work is worth something today because of the thousands of fans on Facebook who send in their valuable comments day in and day out. A big thanks to 'Rang Leela', 'Piyush's Poetry', and 'Lovers of Poetry' fb page fans!

Lastly, I have been very fortunate to have a great team at Notion Press and I would like to thank Naveen, Vandana, Yamini and Santhosh for helping me in making this book a reality.

Prologue

रंग की क्या बात करें,

रंग ही तो है सब कुछ...

बिना रंग क्या है यहाँ पे...

बिना रंग के है क्या कुछ?

Rang ki kya baat karein...

Rang hi to hai sab kuch

Bina rang kya hai yahan pe...

Bina rang ke hai kya kuch

Life is all about the various experiences and personalities that one comes across. Each experience or interaction shapes the way we think, feel and do things. These experiences form the colours of our lives. And that's everything we are all about!

Let's experience some of these colours!

Contents

Hindi Poems

Couplets

English Poems

Hindi Poems

(with transliteration)

बचपन की वो कागज़ की कश्ती

बारिश के पानी से समंदर तक,

छोटी चुनौतियों से बड़े बवंडर तक,

मीलों का सफ़र तय कर आई है...

बचपन की वो कागज़ की कश्ती, काफ़ी दूर चल आई है |

❋❋❋

लहरों से स्थिरता, मकामों से उम्मीद,

तूफानों से साहस लिए,

अनुभवों की बुनियाद पे हमेशा कुछ नया सीखती आई है...

बचपन की वो कागज़ की कश्ती, काफ़ी दूर चल आई है |

❋❋❋

बहुत मिले राह में साथी हमसफर,

थोड़ी देर साथ चले, फिर थामी अपनी डगर,

कुछ को साथ लिए, कुछ को पीछे छोड़ आई है...

बचपन की वो कागज़ की कश्ती, काफ़ी दूर चल आई है |

❋❋❋

मंजिल कहाँ है, मालूम नहीं,

पर पाना है उसे, इतना है यकीन,

शायद यही सोच के अब तक बढ़ती आई है...

बचपन की वो कागज़ की कश्ती, काफ़ी दूर चल आई है।

Bachpan ki woh kagaz ki kashti

Baarish ke paani se samandar tak,

Chhoti chunautiyon se bade bavandar tak,

Meelon ka safar tay kar aayi hai...

Bachpan ki woh kagaz ki kashti, kafi door chal aayi hai

❋❋❋

Lehron se sthirta, makamon se umeed,

Toofanon se saahas liye,

Hamesha kuch naya seekhti aayi hai...

Bachpan ki woh kagaz ki kashti, kafi door chal aayi hai

❋❋❋

Bahut mile raah mein saathi humsafar,

Kuch der saath chale, phir thaami apni dagar,

Kuch ko saath liye, kuch ko peeche chhor aayi hai...

Bachpan ki wo kagaz ki kashti kafi door chal aayi hai

❋❋❋

Manzil kahan hai, maaloom nahin,

Par paana hai use, itna hai yakeen,

Shayad yahi soch ke ab tak badti aayi hai...

Bachpan ki wo kagaz ki kashti, kafi door chal aayi hai

इश्क़

इश्क़ क्या है? ... क्या यह सिर्फ महबूब के लिए प्यार है या उससे ज़्यादा....क्या यह सिर्फ दो लोगों के दरमियां है या यह है हर जगह...

इश्क़ हर जगह है,
हर जगह इश्क़ है,
ज़िन्दगी को 'ज़िन्दगी' देने वाला...
और कुछ नहीं, बस इश्क़ है!

जो नहीं कर सकते,
उसी को करने के सपने दिन रात देखते हैं...
यह अनहोनी को होनी में बदलने की आस...
और कुछ नहीं, बस इश्क़ है!

कोई कर के सीखना चाहता है,
कोई सीख के करना चाहता है,
यह जुनून कुछ कर गुज़रने का...
और कुछ नहीं, बस इश्क़ है!

कल गले लगाया था जिसे,
उसी से आज तकरार होती है...
यह अपनों से नफरतों का वजूद...
और कुछ नहीं, बस इश्क़ है!

***

कोई मंदिरों में ढूंढ़ता है,
कोई मस्जिदों में तलाशता है,
यह रूहानियत की लम्बी खोज...
और कुछ नहीं, बस इश्क़ है!

***

इश्क़ हर जगह है,
हर जगह इश्क़ है...
ज़िन्दगी को 'ज़िन्दगी' देने वाला...
और कुछ नहीं, बस इश्क़ है!

***

Ishq

Ishq kya hai? ... kya yeh sirf mehboob ke liye pyaar hai ya usse zyaada...kya yeh sirf do logon ke darmiyan hai ya yeh hai har jagah...

Ishq har jagah hai,

Har jagah ishq hai,

Zindagi ko 'zindagi' dene waala...

Aur kuch nahi, bas ishq hai!

***

Jo nahi kar sakte,

Usi ko karne ke sapne din raat dekhte hain...

Yeh anhoni ko honi mein badalne ki aas...

Aur kuch nahi, bas ishq hai!

***

Koi kar ke seekhna chahta hai,

Koi seekh ke karna chahta hai,

Yeh junoon kuch kar guzarne ka...

Aur kuch nahi, bas ishq hai!

Kal gale lagaya tha jisse,

Ussi se aaj takraar hoti hai...

Yeh apnon se nafraton ka wajood...

Aur kuch nahi, bas ishq hai!

Koi mandiron mein dhoondta hai,

Koi masjidon mein talashta hai,

Yeh roohaniyat ki lambi khoj...

Aur kuch nahi, bas ishq hai!

Ishq har jagah hai,

Har jagah ishq hai...

Zindagi ko 'zindagi' dene waala...

Aur kuch nahi, bas ishq hai!

❋❋❋

विचारधारा

अगर सत्य से हमेशा असत्य है हारा...
और सब कुछ होता सिर्फ गोरा या काला...
तो क्या अब तक बह रही होती यह धारा?
यह तुम्हारी हमारी विचारधारा |

***

एक-जुट हुए जिससे सभी ...
बनी यह हक़ की एक लड़ाई
विभाजित भी उसी ने किया...
और फसादों की जड़ कहलाई |

***

जीवन में किसी ने अपनाई...
तो उसूलों में उनके नज़र आई
किसी ने इस्तमाल की...
तो बनी यह सियासत की चढ़ाई |

***

भेदभाव ना करती...
सबकी है, अपनी अपनी यह सबको प्यारी
एक करके अलग करने की क्षमता रखती...
निर्बल यह बेचारी |

***

कोई गांधी की पूजा करता...
तो कोई हिंसा को सही ठहराता है
कोई कहता कि गलत ने है सही को मारा...
तो कोई मानता है इन्हे सिर्फ दो अलग विचारधारा |

***

अगर सत्य से हमेशा असत्य है हारा...
और सब कुछ होता सिर्फ गोरा या काला...
तो क्या अब तक बह रही होती यह धारा?
यह तुम्हारी हमारी विचारधारा |

***

VICHAARDHARA

Agar satya se hamesha asatya hai haara...
Aur sab kuch hota sirf gora ya kaala...
To kya ab tak beh rahi hoti yeh dhaara?
Yeh tumhari hamari vichaardhaara.

❋❋❋

Ek-jut hue jisse sabhi ...
Bani yeh hakk ki ek ladai
Vibhajit bhi usi ne kiya...
Aur phasaadon ki jad kehlaai.

❋❋❋

Jeevan mein kisi ne apnaayi...
To usoolon mein unke nazar aayi
Kissi ne istmaal ki...
To bani yeh siyaasat ki chaddaai.

❋❋❋

Bhedbhaav na karti...

Sabki hai, apni apni yeh sabko pyaari

Ek karke alag karne ki shamta rakhti...

Nirbal yeh bechaari.

***

Koi Gandhi ki pooja karta...

To koi Hinsa ko sahi thehrata hai

Koi kehta ki galat ne hai sahi ko maara...

To koi maanta hai inhe sirf do alag vichaardhaara.

***

Agar satya se hamesha asatya hai haara...

Aur sab kuch hota sirf gora ya kaala...

To kya ab tak beh rahi hoti yeh dhaara?

Yeh tumhari hamari vichaardhaara.

***

कि महफ़िल हँस पड़ेगी

1948 - महात्मा

ना बताओ इन्हें कि,
कोई था सच का पुजारी...
कि महफ़िल हँस पड़ेगी,
तुम्हे समझ के अनाड़ी...

❋❋❋

1931 - भगत सिंह

ना बताओ इन्हें कि,
किसी ने दी थी देश के लिए जान की कुर्बानी...
कि महफ़िल हँस पड़ेगी,
सुनकर तुम्हारी यह नादानी...

❋❋❋

1857 - मंगल पांडे

ना बताओ इन्हें कि,
किसी एक ने आज़ादी पाने की थी ठानी...
कि महफ़िल हँस पड़ेगी,
पूछेगी तुम्हारी क्या है परेशानी...

***

ना बताओ इन्हें कि,
महफ़िल उनके लायक या वह महफ़िल के लायक नहीं...
वो तो थे वीर, कुछ अलग जज़बाती,
यह महफ़िल मतलबी उन्हें क्या ख़ाक अपनाती...

***

क्या हम इन क्रांत्कारियों के लायक थे? क्या हमारा समाज कभी इन विचारधाराओं को समझ पाया? क्यों हमने इन सब को भुला दिया? इन जैसे वीर अब क्यों जन्म नहीं लेते?

Ki Mehfil Hass Padegi

1948 - The Mahatama

Na batao inhe ki,

Koi tha sach ka pujaari...

Ki mehfil hass padegi,

Tumhe samajh ke anari...

1931 - Bhagat Singh

Na batao inhe ki,

Kisi ne di thi desh ke liye jaan ki kurbaani...

Ki mehfil hass padegi,

Sunkar tumhaari yeh naadaani...

1857 - Mangal Pandey

Na batao inhe ki,

Kisi ek ne aazadi paane ki thi thaani...

Ki mehfil hass padegi,

Poochegi tumhaari kya hai pareshaani...

Na batao inhe ki,

Mehfil unke layak ya woh mehfil ke layak nahi...

Woh to the veer, kuch alag jazbaati,

Yeh mehfil matlabi unhe kya khaak apnaati...

Kya hum in krantikariyon ke layak the? Kya hamara samaaj kabhi in vichaardharaon ko samajh paaya? Kyun humne in sab ko bhula diya? In jaise veer ab kyun janm nahi lete?

हमदम

तेरे मदमस्त प्यालों के नशे में...
कुछ संभल सा जाता हूँ मैं

❋❋❋

तेरी महक के मदहोश एहसास में...
कुछ जुनून सा महसूस करता हूँ मैं

❋❋❋

तेरी चुस्कियों के पलों में...
कुछ जीवन सा जी लेता हूँ मैं

❋❋❋

तेरी सुस्त नरम गर्माहट में...
कुछ जोश सा पाता हूँ मैं

❋❋❋

कभी सोचता हूँ कि तुम ना होती...
तो कौन होता मेरे संघर्षों में हमदम

❋❋❋

फिर तुम्हे लबों से लगा के...

कुछ खो सा जाता हूँ मैं

***

कुछ रिश्ते जो हमेशा के लिए होते हैं. वो समय के साथ और भी बेहतर हो जाते हैं. एक ऐसे ही रिश्ते को समर्पित.

Humdum

Tere madmastt pyalon ke nashe mein...

Kuchh sambhal sa jaata hun main

❋❋❋

Teri mehak ke madhosh ehsaas mein...

Kuchh junoon sa mehsoos karta hun main

❋❋❋

Teri chuskiyon ke palon mein...

Kuchh jeevan se jee leta hun main

❋❋❋

Teri sustt naram garmahat mein...

Kuchh josh sa paata hun main

❋❋❋

Kabhi sochta hun ki tum na hoti...

To kaun hota mere sangharshon mein Humdum

❋❋❋

Phir tumhe labbon se laga ke...

Kuchh kho sa jaata hun main

❋❋❋

Kuch rishte jo hamesha ke liye hote hain. Woh samay ke saath aur bhi behtar ho jaate hain. Ek aise hi rishte ko samarpit.

ज़िन्दगी

कहीं अरमानों की उडान...
कहीं निराशा की गहरी शाम है ज़िन्दगी

***

कहीं खुश और आज़ाद...
कहीं हालातों की गुलाम है ज़िन्दगी

***

कहीं उसूलों की मिसाल...
कहीं ईमानों का भद्दा बाज़ार है ज़िन्दगी

***

कहीं बेखौफ़ बुलन्द आवाज़...
कहीं सिमटी हुई सिसकियाँ लेती चुप-चाप है ज़िन्दगी

***

कहीं शौहरत और चमक-दमक...
कहीं लाखों मे गुमनाम है ज़िन्दगी

***

कहीं सीधी-साधी...
कहीं हर पल एक उल्झा सवाल है ज़िन्दगी

***

कहाँ सभी को एक-सा मिला है...
मेरी कुछ, तुम्हारी कुछ और है ज़िन्दगी...

***

ZINDAGI

Kahin armaanon ki udaan...

Kahin niraasha ki gehri sham hai zindagi

❋❋❋

Kahin khush aur aazad...

Kahin haalaton ki ghulam hai zindagi

❋❋❋

Kahin usulon ki misaal...

Kahin eemanon ka bhadda baazar hai zindagi

❋❋❋

Kahin bekhauf buland aawaz...

Kahin simti hui siskiyaan leti chup-chaap hai zindagi

❋❋❋

Kahin shauhrat aur chamak-damak...

Kahin laakhon mein gumnaam hai zindagi

❋❋❋

Kahin seedhi-saadhi...

Kahin har pal ek uljha sawaal hai zindagi

***

Kahan sabhi ko ek-sa mila hai...

Meri kuch, tumhari kuch aur hai zindagi

***

रंग लीला

रंग की क्या बात करें,
रंग ही तो है सब कुछ...
बिना रंग क्या है यहाँ पे...
बिना रंग के है क्या कुछ?

***

रंग बहा है सरहद पे...
वो नीले ऊँचे पर्वत पे
कि रंग उतरा है मांगों से...
वो रंगीन चूड़ीदार हाथों से

***

रंग मिला है माटी में...
वो माँ की पावन छाती में
रंग निकला घर की किलकारियों से...
वो लाली नन्हे गालों से

***

कि आज तक वो पगली शहादत समझ ना पायी थी...

उम्मीद के रंग से फिर अपनी मांग सजाई थी

बिखरी थी...मची तबाही थी...

जब सरकारी मुआवज़े की खबर घर आई थी

सेना के जवानों को समर्पित

Rang Leela

Rang ki kya baat karein,
Rang hi to hai sab kuch...
Bina rang kya hai yahan pe...
Bina rang ke hai kya kuch?

Rang baha hai sarhad pe...
Woh neele unche parbat pe
Ki rang uttra hai maangon se...
Woh rangeen churidaar haathon se

Rang mila hai maati mein...
Woh maa ki paavan chhaati mein
Rang nikla ghar ki kilkariyon se...
Woh laali nanhe gaalon se

Ki aaj tak woh pagli shahadat samajh na paayi thi...
Umeed ke rang se phir apni maang sajayi thi
Bikhri thi...machi tabahi thi...
Jab sarkari muavze ki khabar ghar aayi thi

***

Sena ke jawaanon ko samarpit

जाने कल क्या ले आये

जाने कल क्या ले आये...
जाने क्या पीछे छूट जाये

***

आज थाम ले ... जो भी है तेरा...
आज छोड़ दे... जो अपना न हुआ..

***

आज बोल दे... जो है अनकहा...
आज छुपा ले... जो है बस तेरा...

***

आज वो कर... जो कभी ना किया...
आज रोक ले... जो यह हाथ है उठा...

***

आज सोच ले... जो हो कुछ नया...
आज भूल जा... जो है हो चुका...

***

आज आग बना... जो अरमान है तेरे...

आज सींच दे... जो बंजर हो चुका...

❋❋❋

आज जीत ले... जो बाज़ी हार चुका...

आज हार जा... जो है सब तेरा...

❋❋❋

जाने कल क्या ले आये...

जाने क्या पीछे छूट जाये

❋❋❋

आज ही सब कुछ है...सब कुछ आज है... वो करो जो तुम करना चाहते हो... जाने कल क्या ले आये

Jaane kal kya le aaye

Jaane kal kya le aaye...
Jaane kya peechhe chhoot jaye

Aaj thaam le... jo bhi hai tera...
Aaj chhod de... jo apna na hua..

Aaj bol de... jo hai unkaha...
Aaj chhupa le... jo hai bas tera...

Aaj woh kar... jo kabhi na kiya...
Aaj rok le... jo yeh haath hai utha...

Aaj soch le... jo ho kuch naya...
Aaj bhool ja... jo hai ho chuka...

Aaj aag bana... jo armaan hai tere...
Aaj seench de... jo banjar ho chuka...

Aaj jeet le... jo baazi haar chuka...
Aaj haar ja... jo hai sab tera...

Jaane kal kya le aaye...
Jaane kya peeche chhoot jaye

Aaj hi sab kuch hai...sab kuch aaj hai... Woh karo jo tum karna chahte ho...
jaane kal kya le aaye

इस कदर

यूँ रहा तो मैं हूँ कई जगह...
इस कदर कहीं ठहराव नहीं हुआ...
यूँ मिला तो हूँ मैं कइयों से...
इस कदर कभी लगाव नहीं हुआ...

❋❋❋

यूँ बोला तो मैं हूँ काफी कुछ...
इस कदर कभी शब्द अल्फ़ाज़ नहीं हुआ...
यूँ चाहा तो है मैंने भी कभी कभी...
इस कदर इश्क़ का एहसास नहीं हुआ...

❋❋❋

यूँ छोटी गलतियां भी हुई काफी मुझसे...
इस कदर गुस्ताखियों का आभास नहीं हुआ...

❋❋❋

Is kadar

Yun raha to main hun kai jagah...
Is kadar kahin thehraav nahi hua...

Yun mila to hun main kaiyon se...
Is kadar kabhi lagaav nahi hua...

Yun bola to main hun kafi kuch...
Is kadar kabhi shabd alfaaz nahi hua...

Yun chaha to hai maine bhi kabhi kabhi...
Is kadar ishq ka ehsaas nahi hua...

Yun chhoti galtiyian bhi hui kafi mujhse...
Is kadar gustakhiyon ka aabhas nahi hua...

Couplets

(with transliteration)

ज़ुबां

दायरों में रहे तो...

अदब और मान होती है ..

वरना बे -इज़्ज़त सरे आम होती है ...

ज़ुबां तो आखिर ज़ुबां होती है...

ZUBAAN

Daairon mein rahe to...
Adab aur maan hoti hai..
Varna be-izzat sare-aam hoti hai...
Zubaan to aakhir zubaan hoti hai...

रिश्ते नाते

सब चले जायेंगे...
ये दो पल के मेहमान
कुछ बोल रह जायेंगे...
बनके जिस्म-ओ-जान

सब नाते टूट जायेंगे...
ये तो बस कच्चे मकान
कुछ रिश्ते रह जायेंगे...
बनके तेरा जहाँ

Rishte Naate

Sab chale jayenge...
Yeh do pal ke mehman
Kuch bol reh jayenge...
Banke jism-o-jaan

Sab naate toot jayenge..
Yeh to bas kacche makan
Kuch rishte reh jayenge...
Banke tera jahan

कलम

सूख गयी अब स्याही इस कलम की ऐ 'जयंत'..
कि कदरदान कम हैं अब इस शौंक के
फिर भी लिख ज़माने में क्या कमी है...
कि यह ज़माना अब भी एक आईने को तरसता है

Kalam

Sookh gayi ab syaahi is kalam ki ae 'jayant'...
Ki kadardaan kam hain ab is shounk ke

Phir bhi likh zamaane mein kya kami hai...
Ki yeh zamaana ab bhi ek aaine ko tarasta hai

फ़ुर्सत के वो पल

फ़ुर्सत के वो चंद पल...
ज़िन्दगी भर की उलझनों के हल
वो कुछ क्षणों का आराम...
वो फिर बोलना 'आज नहीं कल'

Fursat ke wo pal

Fursat ke wo chand pal...
Zindagi bhar ki uljhanon ke hal

Wo kuch kshranon ka aaram...
Wo phir bolna 'aaj nahi kal'

मोड़

आज फिर एक दिलचस्प मोड़ पे आई है ज़िन्दगी...
आज फिर मैं बस सिर्फ सीधा चलना चाहता हूँ

Mod

Aaj phir ek dilchasp mod pe aayi hai zindagi...
Aaj phir main bas sirf seedha chalna chahta hun

नसीब

क्या लिखा है... कौन पढ़ सकता है?
किसकी रज़ा है... कौन जान सकता है?
कब क्या हो... कौन कह सकता है?
नसीबों का खेल... अजब है...
इसे कौन समझ...कौन समझा सकता है?

NASEEB

Kya likha hai... kaun pad sakta hai?
Kiski razza hai... kaun jaan sakta hai?
Kab kya ho... kaun keh sakta hai?
Naseebon ka khel... ajab hai...
Isse kaun samajh...kaun samjha sakta hai?

नज़रिया

न खुशियों की बहार... न ग़मों का दरिया है...
ज़िन्दगी और कुछ नहीं... बस अपना अपना नज़रिया है...

Nazariya

Na khushiyon ki bahaar... Na ghamon ka dariyaa hai...
Zindagi aur kuch nahi... bas apna apna nazariyaa hai...

शब्द

कुछ खो के लिखा...
कुछ पा के लिखा
हमने इस कलम को...
अक्सर आँसुओं में डुबो के लिखा

कभी मिली नसीहत...
कभी वाह-वाही मिली
हमने अपने ग़मों को...
अक्सर शब्दों में संजो के लिखा

Shabd

Kuch kho ke likha...
Kuch paa ke likha
Humne is kalam ko...
Aksar aansuon mein dubo ke likha

Kabhi mili naseehat...
Kabhi wah-wahi mili
Humne apne gamon ko...
Aksar shabdon mein sanjo ke likha

दुआ

मस्तक पे खुशियों का ताज हो...
हाथों से सदा अच्छे काज हों
वाणी में सदैव राम राज हो...
कुछ इस तरह हमेशा आपका आज हो

Dua

Mastak pe khushiyon ka taj ho...
Haathon se sada achhe kaaj hon
Vani mein sadaiv raam raaj ho...
Kuch is tarah hamesha aapka aaj ho

दूरियां

यूँ दिलों में दूरियां न थीं..

लफ़्ज़ों की मजबूरियां न थीं...

कुछ आँखें बात कर लेती थीं..

कुछ खामोशियाँ बयां कर देती थीं...

आज बोलते हो तुम... तो सुनाई देता है...

पर धड़कनें वो रफ़्तार नहीं पकड़तीं...

Dooriyan

Yun dilon mein dooriyan na theen..
Lafzon ki majboorian na theen...

Kuchh ankhein baat kar leti theen...
Kuchh khamoshiyaan byaan kar deti theen...

Aaj bolte ho tum... to sunai deta hai...
Par dharkanein woh raftaar nahi pakadtin...

वफ़ा

कल तुम्हारे ही दर से बेकदर होके रुस्वा हुए थे..
आज तुम फिर किस वफ़ा की बात करते हो...

WAFAA

Kal tumhaare hi darr se bekadar hoke ruswaa hue the..

Aaj tum phir kis wafaa ki baat karte ho...

ग़म

मुस्कुराहटों में छुपा लेता हूँ...

कि कभी चहरे पे नज़र न आए...

लफ़्ज़ों में दफना देता हूँ ...

कि कभी जुबां पे न आ जाए...

पर उनका क्या करूँ...

जो मेरी आँखों से...मेरा ग़म जान लेते हैं...

Gham

Muskurahaton mein chhupa leta hun...
Ki kabhi chehre pe nazar na aaye...

Lafzon mein dafna deta hun...
Ki kabhi zubaan pe na aa jaye...

Par unka kya karun...
Jo meri aankhon se...Mera gham jaan lete hain...

दोस्त

कुछ दोस्त हैं जो तो तुम्हे तुमसे ज़्यादा जाने...
उनका कहा हमेशा सुनें और मानें...

DOST

Kuch dost hai jo to tumhe tumse zyaada jaane...
Unka kaha hamesha sune aur maane...

दिल्ली कि सर्दी

बर्फ़ के मुलायम धुंए में लिपटी तेरी ये सुबहें...
तेरी मदहोशी के आगोश में कटती यह हसीं शामें...
मखमली 'रज़ाई' की वो सुस्त अँगड़ाइयाँ...
चाय के प्यालों का वो नशा...

Dilli ki Sardi

Barff ke mulayam dhuein mein lipti teri yeh subahein...
Teri madhoshi ke aagosh mein kat-ti yeh haseen shaamein...
Makhmali 'razaai' ki woh sust angraaiyan...
Chai ke pyaalon ka wo nashaa...

रुस्वा

आज शब्दों से कुछ हूँ मैं रुस्वा...
कि दिल-ए-ख़ुशी बयां न कर पाएंगे वो

RUSWA

Aaj shabdon se kuch hun main ruswaa...
Ki dil-e-khushi bayaan na kar payenge wo

याराना

ये जो कुछ पल है हमारा अफ़साना...
अभी कल मिले, शायद कल है हमें बिछड़ जाना
मेरी यादों में बस के तू रह जाना...
मेहफ़ूज़ और सलामत रहेगा ये याराना...

Yaarana

Yeh jo kuchh pal hai hamara afsaana...
Abhi kal mile, shayad kal hai hamen bichhad jaana.
Meri yaadon mein bass ke tu reh jaana...
Mehfoos aur salaamat rahega yeh yaarana.

सच

ये कैसा अजब खेला है...
भीड़ में भी क्यों तू अकेला है
बनावटों की गुफ्तगू से क्यों है महफ़िलें रवां...
क्यों है सच्चाई तनहा यहाँ

Sach

Yeh kaisa ajab khela hai...
Bheed mein bhi kyun tu akela hai

Banavaton ki guftagu se kyun hai mehfilein ravaan...
Kyun hai sachaai tanha yahaan

खामोशियाँ

कभी दूरियां मिटाती हैं.....कभी फ़ासलें बढाती हैं ...

ये खामोशियाँ न जानें कितनी बातें करती हैं...

Khamoshiyan

Kabhi dooriyan mitati hain.....kabhi faaslein badati hain...
Yeh khamoshiyaan na jaane kitni baatein karti hain...

जश्न

मत हो मायूस...

कि तेरी दुनिया में आज जश्न नहीं हुआ

देख उनको भी जिनके पास...

सिर्फ ज़हर की सुराही है और गला अभी सूखा है

JASHN

Mat ho maayoos...
Ki teri duniya mein aaj jashn nahin hua

Dekh unko bhi jinke paas...
Sirf zeher ki surahi hai aur gala abhi sookha hai

English Poems

Because I was told

I was told,
To be cold
I was told,
To keep the hold
I was told,
To say what sold

***

But, I tried the reverse,
All to my own curse
Whatever was real,
Was not ideal
Now i know why they say,
You sometimes learn it the hard way

***

I wore the mask,
Up and ready for the task
Kept up the pace,
To win the race

***

Prospered, I toiled,
To fill the unseen void
But my attempts were of no use,
For there was no truce

❋❋❋

Then i stumbled upon the forgotten,
The truth dead and rotten

❋❋❋

I was told,
To help the old
I was told,
To bring everyone to the fold
I was told,
To nurture the mould

❋❋❋

Enlightened I march again,
Oblivious of loss or gain
Without any fear or load,
Because I was told....

***

Published in The Taj Mahal Review, an international journal of poetry in 2012

Someday Somewhere

Someday somewhere you meet someone,
Someone you knew long ago
That one person in a billion,
For you who could all forego

***

Who helped you when you were down,
Made you smile when saw you frown
Believed in you against all odds,
Accompanied you on rough roads

***

Left alone miserable in the rain,
Having lived through that pain
You ask that person,
The reason for the treason

***

You wait with baited breath,

Follows a silence harder than death

Far away you hear some bells,

Come back to reality the dawn yells

The Roof

When they were burning the huts outside,
Bringing down the roofs and orphaning those inside...
Unaware and protected from their wrath,
I understood 'love' in your warmth...

***

When they made a hero out of me,
Irrespective of how ordinary my actions be...
Under your shield, I made the correct choice,
Building my character and maintaining poise...

***

When in everything they saw only my ill,
And inside, I too was losing my will...
Through that tunnel all darkening,
In your caress, i kept walking...

***

My roof, for all your strive,

I owe you much more than my life...

Feel blessed to have you, my roof,

For once GOD's presence needs no worldly proof...

***

Dedicated to people who have done everything in their capacity to help you be what you wanted to be...our Gods on earth

Published in The Taj Mahal Review, an international journal of poetry in 2014

You were there

When I first came into this world,
Too small to remember anything ...
I know, You were there!
In the small world around me...
Celebrating my arrival and,
Telling my mother she was fine...

❋❋❋

Years rolled by while I just slept and cried,
In your tender warm arms...
While my mother, unwilling to leave me back,
Could go out to take on the world...
Assuring her always, You were there!

❋❋❋

I grew up in your caress... years flew,

I had a companion now...

He was too small though,

Smaller than I could have ever been, I thought...

Following year my father was away,

Fighting tough battles I never knew...

Back here...Holding us all together,

You were there!

***

And then it was my companion's turn,

Holding your one finger, to taste the real world,

You accompanied him to his playground...

Telling him to take care and wait for her,

Every day, when the bell rang...

He rushed for the gates,

Right by that tree always, You were there!

***

Dedicated to one of the most cheerful persons i have ever met...my late grandmother...RIP